CORE LIBRARY OF US STATES

Kentucky

D1518816

BY L. C. EDWARDS

CONTENT CONSULTANT
Paul A. Tenkotte, PhD
Professor of History
Northern Kentucky University

Core Library

An Imprint of Abdo Publishing
abdobooks.com

abdobooks.com

Published by Abdo Publishing, a division of ABDO, PO Box 398166, Minneapolis, Minnesota 55439.
Copyright © 2023 by Abdo Consulting Group, Inc. International copyrights reserved in all countries.
No part of this book may be reproduced in any form without written permission from the publisher.
Core Library™ is a trademark and logo of Abdo Publishing.

Printed in the United States of America, North Mankato, Minnesota.
052022
092022

Cover Photo: Shutterstock Images, map and icons, baseball bat; Tetiana Babinich/Shutterstock
Images, racehorses
Interior Photos: Robin Alam/Icon Sportswire/Getty Images, 4–5, 45; Red Line Editorial, 7, 7; Leonid
Andronov/Shutterstock Images, 9; Nagel Photography/Shutterstock Images, 12–13; Sarin Images//
Granger Historical Picture Archive, 15; Shutterstock Images, 18 (flag), 18 (horse); Bonnie Taylor Barry/
Shutterstock Images, 18 (bird); Przemyslaw Muszynski/Shutterstock Images, 18 (flower); Natalya
Kokhanova/Shutterstock Images, 18 (coal); Ivelin Denev/Shutterstock Images, 20; Anthony Heflin/
Shutterstock Images, 22–23; Jahi Chikwendiu/The Washington Post/Getty Images, 26; All Canada
Photos/Alamy, 28; Alexey Stiop/Shutterstock Images, 30–31; Everett Collection/Shutterstock Images,
35, 43; PA Images/Getty Images, 36–37; AP Images, 40

Editor: Katharine Hale
Series Designer: Joshua Olson

Library of Congress Control Number: 2021951390

Publisher's Cataloging-in-Publication Data

Names: Edwards, L. C., author.
Title: Kentucky / by L. C. Edwards
Description: Minneapolis, Minnesota : Abdo Publishing, 2023 | Series: Core library of US states |
      Includes online resources and index.
Identifiers: ISBN 9781532197581 (lib. bdg.) | ISBN 9781098270346 (ebook)
Subjects: LCSH: U.S. states--Juvenile literature. | Southeastern States--Juvenile literature. | Kentucky--
      History--Juvenile literature. | Physical geography--United States--Juvenile literature.
Classification: DDC 976.9--dc23

Population demographics broken down by race and ethnicity come from the 2019 census estimate.
Population totals come from the 2020 census.

CONTENTS

CHAPTER ONE
The Bluegrass State 4

CHAPTER TWO
History of Kentucky 12

CHAPTER THREE
Geography and Climate 22

CHAPTER FOUR
Resources and Economy 30

CHAPTER FIVE
People and Places 36

Important Dates. 42

Stop and Think. 44

Glossary. 46

Online Resources 47

Learn More 47

Index 48

About the Author. 48

THE BLUEGRASS STATE

t is the first Sunday in May. More than 150,000 people gather in the stands at Churchill Downs. Many of the women wear large, colorful hats. The Kentucky Derby is about to begin. Twenty horses are led one by one into the long gate. The riders, called jockeys, sit on the tall, powerful horses. The riders wear helmets and brightly colored jackets called silks.

When the horses are in the gate, the crowd goes quiet. The gate doors in front

Justify and jockey Mike Smith, *center*, won the 2018 Kentucky Derby. Justify won two other major horse races that year to become the thirteenth Triple Crown winner in history.

PERSPECTIVES

RETIRED LIFE

Thoroughbred horses that can breed are usually retired from racing by age three. Horses that can't breed are usually raced a little longer. What happens to racehorses after they retire can vary. Successful racehorses often go to breeding farms. Breeders work to create the next generation of champions. Others are retrained for show jumping, ranching, and more. Lucinda Lovitt works for a company that raises money for Thoroughbred aftercare. She said, "We all have a responsibility to provide aftercare. These horses [have] another 25 years of really quality life to give to another family, another sport, another discipline."

of each horse open, and the starting bell rings! The horses leap forward, pounding down the dirt track. People in the crowd shout for their favorite horse to run faster. The race is only 1.25 miles (2 km) long, and it is finished in just over two minutes. It is the longest-running sporting event in the United States, held every year since 1875. Watching the Kentucky Derby is one of the many things to do in Kentucky.

MAP OF
KENTUCKY

Kentucky has many important features and landmarks. How does this map help you understand all that Kentucky has to offer?

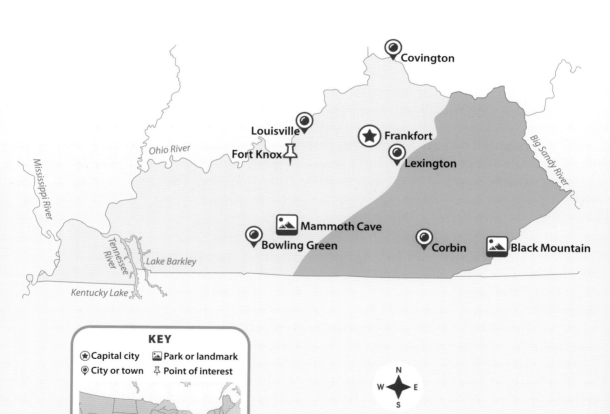

Covington

Louisville

Fort Knox

Frankfort

Lexington

Ohio River

Mississippi River

Big Sandy River

Mammoth Cave

Bowling Green

Corbin

Black Mountain

Tennessee River

Lake Barkley

Kentucky Lake

KEY

★ Capital city   Park or landmark

City or town   Point of interest

N
W   E
S

Appalachian Mountains

EXPLORING KENTUCKY

Kentucky is in the Upper South region of the United States. It is bordered by seven other states. Tennessee lies along Kentucky's entire southern border. Virginia and West Virginia are to the east. Ohio and Indiana are to the north, and Illinois and Missouri lie to the west.

Kentucky is known as the Bluegrass State. It got this name because of the tall, bluish grass that grows in its northern region. This area of rolling hills is where many Thoroughbred racehorses are raised. If these horses are fast enough, they may one day run in the Kentucky Derby.

Kentucky's borders are created mostly by rivers. The Ohio River flows across the northern border. The Mississippi River flows on the west side. In the east the Big Sandy River separates Kentucky from West Virginia. Only Kentucky's borders with Tennessee and Virginia are not formed by rivers. A number of human-made lakes can also be found in Kentucky, including Kentucky Lake

The John A. Roebling Suspension Bridge connects Covington, Kentucky, with Cincinnati, Ohio. Roebling and his son later built the famous Brooklyn Bridge in New York City.

and Barkley Lake. These long, narrow lakes join at their northernmost points and descend into Tennessee. There are even underground natural lakes and rivers such as those found in Mammoth Cave.

Kentucky has numerous cities. Louisville is on the Indiana border. It is home to Churchill Downs and many museums. Lexington is located in the central part of the state and is home to the University of Kentucky. It is near Frankfort, the state capital. The historic cities of Covington and Newport form the Northern Kentucky metropolitan area at the very north of Kentucky. Covington is joined to Cincinnati, Ohio, by bridges. Near the Tennessee border is Bowling Green.

Beyond the city lights, rolling

LOUISVILLE SLUGGER

Louisville Slugger is a famous brand of baseball bats. They have been made in Louisville since 1884. Visitors can tour the Louisville Slugger Museum and Factory to see how the bats are made. Wooden baseball bats start out as cylinders of wood, roughly the length of a bat. The wood is clamped into a machine called a lathe. As the cylinder spins, slender ribbons of wood are shaved away until the bat emerges. The museum also has Louisville Sluggers that belonged to famous baseball players. Visitors can even hold some bats that belonged to all-stars.

hills turn into mountains. Rural towns take the place of cities. Kentucky has a mix of natural landscapes. On the western border, the ground is mostly flat and close to sea level. But the Appalachian Plateau and the Cumberland Plateau rise much higher in the east. Together they form the Appalachian Mountains. The tallest point in the state is Black Mountain. It is 4,145 feet (1,263 m) above sea level. Each region of the state has something unique to offer.

EXPLORE ONLINE

Chapter One discusses the Kentucky Derby. The website listed below has more information on this subject. Does the website answer any questions you had about the race? Were you surprised by anything you saw?

WHAT ARE THE MOST EXCITING TWO MINUTES IN SPORTS?

abdocorelibrary.com/kentucky

HISTORY OF KENTUCKY

People have lived in what is now Kentucky for thousands of years. Ancestors of today's American Indian peoples are called Paleo-Indians. Paleo-Indians were living in the region by approximately 9500 BCE. This was after the last ice age ended. These people were hunters and gatherers.

By approximately 1000 BCE, the peoples of Kentucky began farming. Farming cultures lived in the northern floodplains because

The rotunda of Kentucky's capitol building features murals that represent Kentucky's past and present.

of the region's fertile soil. When the rivers flooded, nutrient-rich soil was left behind. This made the area good for growing vegetables such as squash and corn. This period of hunting, gathering, and farming lasted into the 1500s CE.

At this time other American Indian nations began coming to the region. Shawnee people came from the north. Cherokee groups came from the south. Iroquois people also came to the area.

EUROPEAN SETTLERS ARRIVE

Spanish and French explorers traveled to the area by river in the 1600s. At first many American Indian peoples welcomed the explorers. But the explorers brought European illnesses with them. Because American Indians could not fight off infections such as smallpox, these diseases killed many people.

What is now Kentucky was largely unsettled when France and England fought the French and Indian War (1754–1763). At that time the area was called Kentucky

European settlers and American Indians clashed as settlers took American Indian lands.

County. Both France and England wanted the game and salt deposits found there. Some American Indian nations fought alongside the French. They wanted to keep British colonists from taking their land. Others fought alongside the British. The British defeated the French. In the Proclamation of 1763, the British agreed that no settlers would move into Kentucky County. The area would remain a hunting ground for American Indian peoples.

By the Revolutionary War (1775–1783), settlers were entering Kentucky County. British troops paid American Indians to fight for the British. After the war, colonists continued to settle lands American Indians had previously lived on and hunted. No reservations of

PERSPECTIVES

STEPHEN BISHOP

Stephen Bishop was 17 years old in 1838. He was enslaved by a lawyer named Franklin Gorin. Gorin sent Bishop into Mammoth Cave. Gorin wanted to turn it into a tourist attraction. But he would need a map. Bishop went in with only an oil lantern. It was his job to crawl through passageways and see what was there. He described the cave as "a grand, gloomy, and peculiar place." Bishop drew the first map of the cave in 1842. He also guided visiting tourists. Today electric lights make the trip easier for the 500,000 people who visit the cave each year.

American Indian lands were made in the state.

SLAVERY AND THE CIVIL WAR

Kentucky became a state on June 1, 1792. It was formed out of the state of Virginia. Kentucky relied heavily on farming. The early settlers brought enslaved Black people to the state to farm tobacco. People who were against slavery, known as abolitionists, worked hard to convince other Americans that slavery was wrong. One Kentucky abolitionist was William Shreve Bailey. He was a newspaper owner and editor. People who supported slavery were angered by Bailey's stance. They set fire to his press.

Slavery had become an important issue across the United States. Northern free states believed slavery should be illegal. Southern states disagreed. The Civil War began in 1861. Southern states fought for the Confederacy. Northern states fought for the Union. Kentucky was caught in the middle. Officially the state was neutral, meaning that the state did not take a side. Kentuckians fought for both the Union and the Confederacy. Both the US and Confederate presidents were born in Kentucky. Abraham Lincoln was the US president. Jefferson Davis was the president of the Confederacy. Kentucky's division was visible at the highest level of the war. The Union won in 1865.

MAKING A LIVING

In the late 1800s, many immigrants from Europe came to America. They were seeking freedom and better

KENTUCKY
QUICK FACTS

Each US state has its own unique history and culture. What do Kentucky's state symbols tell you about the state's culture? Did you find any of Kentucky's state symbols surprising?

Abbreviation: KY
Nickname: The Bluegrass State
Motto: United we stand, divided we fall
Date of statehood: June 1, 1792
Capital: Frankfort
Population: 4,505,836
Area: 40,408 square miles (104,656 sq km)

STATE SYMBOLS

State bird
Northern cardinal

State horse
Thoroughbred

State flower
Goldenrod

State mineral
Coal

economic opportunities. Large numbers of these immigrants settled in the cities along the Ohio River. There they found jobs in factories, stores, and offices. In Europe some American mining companies recruited men to come to eastern Kentucky to work in the coal mines.

During the mid-to-late 1800s, Black people made up 20 percent of Kentucky's population. After the Civil War ended in 1865, slavery was illegal, but Black people faced discrimination from white people. Kentucky was segregated until

MUHAMMAD ALI

Muhammad Ali was born Cassius Marcellus Clay Jr. in 1942. He grew up in Kentucky during segregation. Ali began boxing when he was 12 years old. He quickly moved up through the ranks. Soon he was in the Olympics. Ali won a gold medal. But he was just getting started. Ali boxed differently from other athletes. He moved back from opponents and kept his arms low. These techniques worked for Ali. He captured the heavyweight title on three separate occasions. He successfully defended his title 19 times.

Kentucky's capitol building is in Frankfort.

the 1960s. This meant that Black and white people were separated by law. Black people faced violence from white supremacist groups.

Historically Kentucky farmers grew a lot of tobacco. But in 1964 the US Surgeon General issued an important report. It stated that smoking tobacco was dangerous to people's health. Some Kentucky farmers began focusing on other crops, such as soybeans. While tobacco is declining in importance, Kentucky still produces a lot of it.

Agriculture, mining, and manufacturing played an important role in Kentucky's history. Changes in these industries caused people to move from rural areas to cities. Today auto manufacturing, printing, and the assembly of home appliances are all important in Kentucky. The state continues to change as technology changes.

STATE GOVERNMENT

Like the US government, Kentucky's state government has three branches. Each branch plays a different role, and no branch has more power than another. The legislative branch includes elected officials from across the state. There are 38 senators and 100 representatives. The legislative branch writes and votes on bills that might become law. Bills that pass this branch go on to the executive branch. There the governor can sign the bills into law. The third branch is the judicial branch, which includes all courts in Kentucky. This branch interprets laws.

GEOGRAPHY AND CLIMATE

Kentucky's various landscapes formed across millions of years. The eastern coal fields are hilly and mountainous. This region is part of the Appalachian Highlands. The area formed between 570 million and 250 million years ago, when the region was covered by a sea. Sand, dead sea animals, rocks, and soil dropped to the seafloor. Over time they formed layers that were thousands of feet thick. As tectonic plates moved against each other, the layers

The Appalachian Mountains are found in eastern Kentucky.

BIRD-VOICED TREEFROG

The western region of Kentucky is home to an interesting animal. The bird-voiced treefrog sounds like a tweeting bird and lives in forested wetlands. These amphibians have large eyes and are usually light green with grayish bellies. The treefrogs live high in the trees, coming down closer to the water when it is time for females to lay eggs. Each male frog has a unique call made up of 20 or more whistle-like sounds.

were pushed up. This process took millions of years and formed the stone. The hills and valleys of today formed as streams slowly eroded the stone, carrying small bits of it away.

The Bluegrass and Pennyrile regions are in north-central Kentucky. These regions are named for the plants found there. Bluegrass is a tall grass that covers the gently rolling hills of this fertile region. Pennyrile, or pennyroyal, is a type of mint. The Pennyrile region has many sinkholes and caves. These formed within limestone deposits that developed in the area 300 million years ago.

Eastern and north-central Kentucky are very different from western Kentucky. The Coastal Plain is in the western corner of the state. This area is made up of floodplains with low hills. It sits on the New Madrid Fault. This fault is a group of cracks in Earth's crust that are not visible from Earth's surface. Earth's crust is a thick layer of rock that covers the planet.

Kentucky's landscape has changed over time. Before the Civil War, most of the state was covered in forests. Oak, chestnut,

PERSPECTIVES
INVASIVE SPECIES

An invasive species is a species that is not native to an area and has a negative effect on the native species living there. Early American settlers brought wild pigs to the United States. "They are the perfect invasive species," wildlife biologist Terri Brunjes said. "They are highly intelligent. They have high reproductive rates, no natural predators. They can eat anything, and they can live anywhere. . . . They are one of the greatest natural resource challenges we face." Unlike many states, Kentucky's number of wild pigs is dropping. This is due to a trapping program.

Coal mines have damaged Kentucky's forests. Today environmentalists are working to restore forests on former coal mines.

hickory, and walnut trees grew in Kentucky's mild climate. The lumber industry developed after the war ended. It cut many of these trees down. Today most of the forests are in the mountainous eastern region.

People have worked hard to bring forests back by planting trees.

CLIMATE AND WILDLIFE

Kentucky has many different landscapes, but its climate and mild weather are similar across the state. Temperatures vary between summer and winter. Summers are hot and humid with an average daily high of 85 to 90 degrees Fahrenheit (29–32°C) in July. Cloudy weather is more frequent in winter, when average daily highs range from 39 to 45 degrees Fahrenheit (4–7°C) in January. The amount of snow varies each winter and can come in one large snowfall or several lighter ones. In southern Kentucky there is seldom snow on the ground for more than a week. In Northern Kentucky snow does not often cover the ground for more than two weeks.

Sixteen species of bats live in Kentucky. One of these is the little brown bat. Another is the evening bat. Kentucky's bats shelter in trees, buildings, and caves. At night they hunt for insects to eat. In the winter they

The little brown bat is one of 16 bat species that live in Kentucky.

hibernate or move south. When they hibernate, their hearts slow. Their breathing slows. It looks like they are asleep. Kentucky is also home to deer, elk, and black bears.

STRAIGHT TO THE
SOURCE

Coal mining has hurt many of Kentucky's forests. Patrick Angel is a scientist with the US Department of the Interior. He teaches local Kentuckians how to plant trees and help bring back forests in former mining areas. He said:

> These young people are the hope. I'm hoping that they will see the future for planting trees on mine sites in Appalachia, not only for the people of Appalachia, in regards to, you know, their benefit and the economics of the region, but also for the environment of the planet. I mean, there's no better thing for a young person to do to mitigate climate change than to plant trees.

> Source: Gabriel Popkin. "The Green Miles." *Washington Post Magazine*, 13 Feb. 2020, www.washingtonpost.com. Accessed 7 June 2021.

CONSIDER YOUR AUDIENCE

Adapt this passage for a different audience, such as your principal or friends. Write a blog post conveying this same information for the new audience. How does your post differ from the original text and why?

RESOURCES AND ECONOMY

Kentucky's economy has changed over time. Agriculture continues to be important to Kentuckians. Approximately 50 percent of the state is used as farmland. Additionally, 20 percent of the population is employed in agriculture. Thoroughbred breeding is especially important to Kentucky's economy and the state's identity. Kentuckians are proud of the history of horse racing in the state. In addition to Thoroughbred horses, Kentuckians raise

Horses are an important part of Kentucky's agricultural industry.

chickens and cattle. Food crops are also grown in Kentucky. These include soybeans, corn, and wheat. Kentuckians also grow fruits and vegetables, with tomatoes and apples being leading crops.

SERVICE AND MANUFACTURING

Most of Kentucky's economy is based on the service sector. These people work in health care, including jobs at hospitals. Others work in retail by selling clothing, food, and the other things that people need for day-to-day life. Kentuckians also work for the government. Two US Army bases, Fort Knox and Fort Campbell, employ people too. Fort Knox is a famous base. The US government guards gold there.

Manufacturing is also important. Many manufacturing companies are located in urban areas. For example, car companies have plants in Louisville where workers assemble cars. Additionally, Kentucky's coal is used for making metals for car parts. Kentuckians also manufacture food and tobacco products.

COAL

Coal is a major part of Kentucky's economy. It powers most of the state. Coal from the western fields goes to coal-fired electricity plants. Coal is also found in eastern Kentucky. However, jobs in coal mining are declining. Many states are moving away from coal-powered electricity. This is part of the movement away from pollution-causing fossil fuels. Mining with machines is more effective and less

PERSPECTIVES
FORT KNOX GOLD

Countries around the world keep gold reserves. Paper money changes from country to country. But gold is recognized worldwide. If something happens to paper money, governments can rely on gold. The US government keeps most of its reserve at Fort Knox. Workers sometimes perform audits. They count and weigh the gold bars. Doug Simmons had just finished high school when he got an auditing job at Fort Knox in 1975. He said, "You're going down into the basement . . . and the gold doesn't sparkle, and it isn't fancy. It weighs a ton . . . so the glamor wears off [after] about bar number two."

RENEWABLE ENERGY

Renewable energy is energy collected from wind, water, and sunlight. Seven percent of the electricity used in Kentucky in 2020 was produced by hydroelectric dams. At a hydroelectric dam, water passes through a turbine. The turbine turns and generates electricity. The state has 10 hydroelectric dams. These dams are on the Cumberland, Laurel, Ohio, and Tennessee Rivers.

dangerous for people. But it means miners lose their jobs. Some towns in Kentucky were first built up because of the boom in coal mining. Many people came to the area to work in the mines. When mines shut down, people lose their jobs. The towns struggle to support the people living in them. The federal government pays for programs to help these areas move beyond coal. Abandoned Mine Land Economic Revitalization (AMLER) grants support projects that create jobs on or near abandoned coal mines. One AMLER grant funded a wildlife reserve on an abandoned mine. Another project turned coal

Coal and the mining industry have a long history in Kentucky.

railways into a tourist attraction. In addition, programs such as the eKentucky Advanced Manufacturing Institute (eKAMI) train people for jobs in manufacturing. Many of the students are former coal miners.

FURTHER EVIDENCE

Chapter Four discusses agriculture as part of Kentucky's economy. Identify one of the author's main points. What evidence is provided to support this point? The web page at the link below also gives information on Kentucky's agriculture. Find a quote on this site that adds to the information provided in this book.

QUICK FACTS

abdocorelibrary.com/kentucky

PEOPLE AND PLACES

T he people who live in Kentucky are an ever-changing group. White people who are not Hispanic or Latino make up 84.1 percent of the state's population. Many Black Americans left Kentucky after the Civil War, hoping to escape racial violence by moving north. This movement was called the Great Migration. Today only 8.5 percent of Kentuckians are Black. There are growing populations of Hispanic and Asian people in Kentucky, but less than 4 percent of the

Boxer Muhammad Ali, born Cassius Clay, was from Kentucky.

RAJON RONDO

Rajon Rondo was born in Louisville in 1986. As a young athlete, Rondo played baseball and football. But once he hit high school, he shifted his focus to basketball. Playing for the University of Kentucky, he set a record for the most steals in one season. He was drafted by the Phoenix Suns in 2006 then traded to the Boston Celtics. In 2010 he became the first Celtic to lead the league in steals. He also won the NBA assists title three times. Rondo has played for many NBA teams including the Los Angeles Lakers and Los Angeles Clippers.

population was born in another country. There are no federally recognized American Indian tribes in Kentucky.

Famous Kentuckians include actress Jennifer Lawrence and Olympic sprinter Tyson Gay. Loretta Lynn is a country music singer and songwriter who was born in Butcher Hollow in 1932. She released more than 160 songs and 60 albums and is known for the song "Coal Miner's Daughter." She wrote a memoir of the same name telling about her life in coal country. The book became a *New York Times* best seller.

PLACES

Approximately half of Kentuckians live in one of three metropolitan areas. These are Louisville, Lexington, and Northern Kentucky. Bowling Green is the fourth-largest metropolitan area in Kentucky. People who do not live in cities live in smaller towns and rural areas across the state.

Hiking, fishing, and camping are popular Kentucky activities. Land Between the Lakes National

PERSPECTIVES

BLACK HORSEMEN OF THE KENTUCKY TURF

In March 2020 the International Museum of the Horse at the Kentucky Horse Park debuted a new permanent exhibit. It told about the Black workers involved in early Thoroughbred history. Museum Director Amy Beisel said,

> This exhibit is important because it tells the complete history. . . . The men and sometimes women who cared for the horses, who rode the horses, who exercised the horses, who groomed them, who shod them, who fed them. . . . They were historically African American when the Thoroughbred industry was rising in Kentucky.

Harland Sanders, *right*, started Kentucky Fried Chicken in Corbin, Kentucky.

Recreation Area is between Kentucky Lake and Barkley Lake, stretching into Tennessee. It includes forests and wetlands for picnicking, hiking, fishing, and more.

Kentucky colleges are known for their dedicated basketball fans. Fans gather to cheer on the University of Kentucky Wildcats. Kentucky is also known for food and music. In 1930 Harland Sanders started selling chicken at a gas station in Corbin. Today Kentucky Fried Chicken (KFC) is known around the world. Other specialties include barbecue and butter cake. Kentucky is also the birthplace of bluegrass, a type of country music. From cities to open country, Kentucky has a lot to offer both visitors and the people who live there.

STRAIGHT TO THE
SOURCE

The Appalachian region has a higher poverty rate than the rest of the United States. News anchor and TV journalist Diane Sawyer was born in Glasgow, Kentucky. In an interview about a documentary she did on poverty in Appalachia, Sawyer talked about her Appalachian roots:

> *You don't have to go many generations back before we were up there fighting our way through those passes and trying to make our way down the mountain like everybody else. I'm always so moved by the bravery and the vitality of these essential American fighters. . . . I think that urban poverty, while often crushing and inestimable, doesn't have the isolation [of rural poverty].*

> Source: Matea Gold. "Diane Sawyer Treks Back into Appalachia."
> *Los Angeles Times*, 11 Feb. 2009, www.latimes.com.
> Accessed 20 Aug. 2021.

WHAT'S THE BIG IDEA?
Read the above quote carefully. What is the main idea Sawyer wants people to understand? Why is it hard to be poor in the Appalachian Mountains?

IMPORTANT DATES

9500 BCE
Paleo-Indians hunt and gather in the region of Kentucky.

1600s
French and Spanish explorers come down rivers
into Kentucky.

1754–1763
The French and Indian War takes place.

1792
Kentucky becomes a state.

1861–1865
The Civil War is fought, with Kentuckians fighting for both
the Union and the Confederacy.

1875
The first Kentucky Derby takes place.

1890s
Coal mining booms.

1930
Harland Sanders first sells Kentucky Fried Chicken.

STOP AND THINK

Tell the Tale

Chapter One of this book discusses the Kentucky Derby at Churchill Downs. Imagine you are at the Derby. Write 200 words about the sights, sounds, and smells you experience. How would you choose a favorite horse?

Dig Deeper

After reading this book, what questions do you still have about Kentucky? With an adult's help, find a few reliable sources that can help you answer your questions. Write a paragraph about what you learned.

Take a Stand

Changing how something is done, like how electricity is produced, can affect many people's lives. Burning coal creates pollution. Mining coal harms the land. But no longer using coal means that people lose their jobs. Do you think it is better to keep doing things the old way or to find new ways to do them? Why?

Why Do I Care?

Think about what makes Kentucky special to the United States. How do resources in Kentucky affect your life? Are there places in Kentucky you would like to visit?

GLOSSARY

colonist
someone from another country who comes to live in a new place that their home country has taken control of, even if other people already live there

fertile
rich in nutrients for growing plants

metropolitan area
a large city and the smaller cities surrounding it

reservation
an area of land set aside for American Indian people

rural
having to do with the countryside

segregation
the separation of groups of people based on race, class, or ethnicity

species
a group of animals or plants that are similar and can reproduce

tectonic plates
massive pieces of rock that make up Earth's crust

urban
relating to a city environment

white supremacist
a person who falsely believes white people are better than people of other races

ONLINE RESOURCES

To learn more about Kentucky, visit our free resource websites below.

Visit **abdocorelibrary.com** or scan this QR code for free Common Core resources for teachers and students, including vetted activities, multimedia, and booklinks, for deeper subject comprehension.

Visit **abdobooklinks.com** or scan this QR code for free additional online weblinks for further learning. These links are routinely monitored and updated to provide the most current information available.

LEARN MORE

O'Brien, Cynthia. *Encyclopedia of American Indian History and Culture*. National Geographic, 2019.

Sanderson, Whitney. *Intro to Horse Racing*. Abdo, 2018.

INDEX

agriculture, 6, 13–14, 16, 20–21, 31–32, 35
Ali, Muhammad, 19
American Indians, 13–16, 38
Appalachian Mountains, 7, 11, 23, 29, 41

Bailey, William Shreve, 16–17
bats, 27–28
Bishop, Stephen, 16
bluegrass, 8, 18, 24, 40

Civil War, 16–17, 19, 25, 37
climate, 27, 29

forests, 24, 25–27, 29, 40
Fort Knox, 7, 32, 33
Frankfort, 7, 10, 18

Kentucky Derby, 5–6, 8, 11
Kentucky Fried Chicken (KFC), 40

lakes, 7, 8–9, 39–40
Lawrence, Jennifer, 38
Lexington, 7, 10, 39
Louisville, 7, 10, 32, 39
Lynn, Loretta, 38

Mammoth Cave, 7, 9, 16

manufacturing, 10, 19, 21, 32, 35
mining, 19, 21, 29, 33–35

New Madrid Fault, 25

rivers, 7, 8–9, 14, 19, 34
Rondo, Rajon, 38

segregation, 19–20

Thoroughbred horses, 6, 8, 18, 31, 39

University of Kentucky, 10, 38, 40

About the Author

L. C. Edwards lives and writes in the state of Missouri. She has visited Kentucky numerous times, although she has never been to the Kentucky Derby.